Self Care is so important. Your needs are so important, and you need to take good care of yourself. It helps your confidence, self esteem and helps to build a healthy relationship with yourself.

Self Care will make you feel better about yourself, and promote positivity in your life. When you are a mum, self care can be trickier. Harder to find the time to do it, knowing you've got a million and one other things to do. But don't forget, you are needed. Your child needs you to be there, to be happy, to be strong. They depend on you, and you matter.

Taking that time out just for you, is so important.

The cold weather can take it's toll on all of us, and our mental health. Many of us love the changing seasons, but that doesn't mean it wont be challenging too, particularly if you struggle with seasonal depression or holiday related anxiety.

Ensuring you carve out time for yourself and practise self care can make a huge difference on your mental and physical health.

I've got 100 different ideas for self care in this little book, but I just want you to remember - this isn't a *checklist. The most important thing is you taking time out for you. Do things you enjoy and make you feel good about yourself.* xx

www.whimsicalmumblings.co.uk

# Watch A Christmas Movie

Pop on your favourite Christmas movie and get snuggly under a blanket. Pj's and a hot drink almost essential!

# Make your home smell festive

Light a scented candle, fill up your oil burner or pop a pot of festive spice pot pourri on the stove!

# Make a playlist of your favourite Winter songs

They don't have to be only Christmas songs either - as long as they put you in a good mood!

# Keep your body healthy

Ensure you are drinking enough water, getting enough sleep. Have your flu jab if needed and get an annual check up.

# Make a homemade gift

For you or for a loved one!
Homemade gifts are the best, so
much more thought and effort are
put in to them.

# Decorate for Christmas

Sprinkle some Christmas fairy dust, add some twinkly lights and a few snowflakes – or go all out it you'd prefer!

# Wrap up warm and go for a walk

Pop on a coat, hat, gloves, scarf and boots & get yourself some Vitamin D

# Enjoy a hot bubbly bath

Use lots of bubble bath,
essential oils & those bath
bombs you've been 'saving for a
special occasion'

# Draw a little holiday scene

Get your colouring pencils out and draw a cute little holiday scene?

# Write a letter to yourself

Write a letter to yourself to open on New Years Day. Write about the lovely little things that have happened during the year, and what to look forward to in the new year.

# Drink a cup of fancy hot chocolate

Treat yourself to a hot chocolate that's a little more special than your usual drink. Maybe add some whipped cream and marshmallows too!

# Put up some twinkly lights

There's no better time to make your home more cosy. Put up a few twinkly lights in your home to create a lovely & relaxed atmosphere.

# Mo'sterise your whole body

Treat yourself to a fancier, high quality moisteriser and use it all over.

# Bake something delicious

Whether it's a gooey chocolate cake, a christmas pudding, cookies - whatever you fancy, bake a lot of it!

# Enjoy a hot bowl of soup

Homemade or store bought -
enjoy a filling, healthy bowl of joy.

# Try some yoga stretches

If you're new to yoga, why not give a few easy beginner moves a go? Learn to stretch and strengthen your muscles, you may find out you love it!

# Put away your Summer clothes

Have a bit of a clear out, and put away your Summer clothes. It's cosy season!

# Get out your Winter clothes

Get out your Winter clothes! Have a sort through and plan some gorgeous outfit ideas for the chillier months ahead.

# Snuggle up by the fire

Grab some cosy blankets, get snuggly and warm up by a real fire.

# Read a good book

Whether it's your favourite book, a new one you've been putting off reading, or even a motivational non-fiction book.

# Colour in a seasonal colouring page

Get your colouring pencils out and colour in a seasonal colouring page! (Either find one on Pinterest, or use a colouring book).

# Relax by candlelight

Dim the lights and light a few
candles, scented or not and
really relax in the calming light.

# Make a comfy, cosy spot or a pillow fort

Create a comfy spot full of pillows, cushions and blankets, or go all out and make a pillow fort with your little ones- then get snuggled!

# Take a midday nap

If there's one things mums always need, it's more sleep! A midday nap can be just what you need to catch up on sleep again.

# Spend a day in your Pyjamas

Somedays you just don't want to get dressed! Embrace that. Wear your pj's, slippers and dressing gown all day!

# Write a heartfelt letter to a friend or loved one

You can't beat a handwritten, personal letter. Write one to someone you love, or miss, they'd love it.

# Treat yourself to some new, high quality pyjamas

We all deserve a treat now and then, why not treat yourself to some gorgeous snuggly new pyjamas this Winter.

# Have a pampering session

Pluck your brows, shave your legs, have a long soak in the bath. Whatever you fancy, spoil yourself!

# Do a face mask

Whether it's storebought, or natural and homemade - spend some time relaxing with a good facemask on. Cucumber on eyes is essential!

# Paint your nails

Paint your nails a vibrant or festive colour, or even go all out and give yourself a full blown manicure.

# Dance like nobody's watching

Pop on your favourite song and have a loud and proud living room/kitchen dance party!

# Call a friend

Check in on one of your very best friends. Have a long chat and catch up!

# Make a gratitude list

Start a gratitude list of every little thing you are thankful for this year - you'll soon start to realise, there's a lot.

# Start a new hobby

Hobbies are great, as they not only provide you with a chance to switch off, but it means you can focus on something for yourself. Do some research and try out a new hobby.

# Hang up some photos in your home

Whether it's family photos, artwork or motivational quotes (there are some great freebies on Pinterest)! Brighten up your home a little bit this WInter.

# Make a themed collage or vision board

Time to get creative again! Put together a vision board for your dreams and goals, or create a pretty themed collage!

# Make a homecooked meal

Whip up a healthy, hearty homecooked meal to fill you up on this chilly Winter day!

# Rewatch your favourite TV show

Snuggle up and binge watch your favourite TV show today.

# Go for a photo walk

Grab your camera or your phone, wrap up warm and go for a walk - notice and take photos of all the beautiful things you can see.

# Laugh, a lot

Watch a funny movie, laugh with your friends, watch funny Youtube videos today. Anything that will make you laugh until your stomach hurts!

# Create a cosy sanctuary

Change your bedding and turn your bed into a cosy sanctuary! I'm talking blankets, cushions, hot water bottles and fairy lights!

# Buy a fresh bouquet of flowers

Treat yourself to a gorgeous, fresh bunch of flowers today. They'll brighten up your mood *and* your home!

# Write a poem

Give poem writing today. Grab some inspiration from a story, a painting, the weather or even the view from your window!

# Have a digital detox

Try and give yourself a 24 hour digital detox today - it can do wonders for your wellbeing and there's nothing on there that cant wait until tomorrow.

# Listen to a motivating podcast

There are so many podcasts or audio books out there right now, have a browse and find something you'll enjoy. Sit back, relax and listen.

# Hug Someone

Give someone (or yourself) a
huge, loving bear hug today.

# Pop on a hair mask

Give your hair some love today and pop on a luxury, conditioning hair mask.

# Plan 3 things to achieve

Plan 3 things you'd like to achieve over the next 12 months. Big or small, all dreams are welcome!

# Create a new Winter bedtime routine

A good bedtime routine is essential when it comes to looking after yourself. Switch up your routine for the chillier months.

You can't pour from an empty cup

# Write down some of your favourite quotes

Jot down some of your favourite motivational quotes to give yourself a real boost of inspiration.

# Get a massage

Treat yourself and go for a massage, or give yourself one at home.

# Try Meditation

Try giving meditation a go today. I personally recommend the apps 'Headspace' or 'Calm'

# Go to bed early tonight

Sleep is hugely important. Why not give your body a rest and go to bed early tonight!

# Create something

It's time to get creative! Draw a picture, take some photos, paint a picture, build a table, bake a cake – the opportunities are endless.

# Clear your social media

Go through your social media and unfollow people who don't make you happy!

# Observe Nature

Find a quiet spot to sit, and simply watch the beautiful nature all around you.

# Have a slow day

Today is a day to take it easy.
Don't rush around at all. Relax,
unwind and spend time with loved
ones.

# Play

Today is for playing. Whether it's
a card game, a computer game,
a board game with your family,
or toys with your little ones.

# Watch a feel good movie

Unwind and watch a feel good movie today. A movie that really makes you feel *something*.

# Focus on your breathing

Focus your attention on your breath. Inhale and exhale. Observe each breath, the sensation through your nostrils and the rising and falling of your chest.

# Take yourself on a date

Go for a meal or a drink or just
visit somewhere new.

# Declutter

Organise and declutter one space in your home today – whether it's a drawer, a basket, or a whole room!

# Get dressed up

Find that gorgeous outfit you've been saving for a special occasion – every day is special. Do your make up and your hair. You deserve to feel amazing!

# Turn your alarm off

Turn your alarm off tonight and wake up when your body is ready. Many of us don't actually get the correct amount of sleep our body needs, so it's time for a catch up!

# Try a new recipe

Why not give a new recipe a go tonight? Perhaps one you've really been meaning to try but haven't found the time?

# Give yourself an 'at home foot spa treatment'

Soak your feet, maybe using a peppermint lotion. Exfoliate, pop on a foot mask, moisturise and give yourself a pedicure!

# Eat chocolate

Did you know, dark chocolate has lots of beneficial nutrients and antioxidants! Plus, it's physically impossible to feel bad when you're eating chocolate!

# Rearrange your home

I don't know about you, but I always feel so refreshed after i've rearranged my home a little bit! Move the sofa to a different spot, put your bed at the opposite end of your room – the opportunities are endless!

# Learn something new

Use online tutorials or books to teach yourself something new! Whether it's how to sew a button, calligraphy or how to use Photoshop!

# Read a magazine

Sit down, with a cuppa and read a good magazine from cover to cover - maybe even treat yourself to a new one!

# Do an act of kindness

Buy a coffee for a stranger, call your friend, leave a note in a library book, say please and thank you – being kind is easy.

# Do a jigsaw puzzle

Puzzles are great as they are not only relaxing, but they are a great way to boost brain power and concentration, not to mention the sense of achievment you feel when you complete it!

# Read your favourite childhood books

I recently reread all my childhood books with my children and it was lovely to see they enjoyed them just as much as me! Whether you like Roald Dahl or classic Winnie the Pooh, it'll give you a lovely warm feeling in your heart, rereading them.

# Forgive those who have wronged you

Holding onto resentment and anger is not good for you or your mental wellbeing. So let go of those bad feelings and forgive those who have wronged you in the past. Maybe even write (but don't send) a letter of forgiveness to them.

# Eat your favourite meal

Cook or order in your absolute favourite meal today! Whether it's something really fancy, or it's chicken nuggets and potato smiles!

# Make something for you

A relaxing facemask, a fancy hot chocolate, a painting or a scarf! Whatever it is you fancy doing, or whatever you're good at, make it for *you* today!

# Sit and chat with your family/friends

Whatever your plans are today, take some time out and sit down with those closest to you. Share some snacks or a cup of tea and just talk!

# Sing at the top of your lungs

Singing loud and proud, particularly if it's your favourite song, or one you know all the words too!

(One of my favourite ways to cheer myself up is to sing Disney songs *very loud!*)

# Exfoliate

Grab a good, high quality
exfoliator or make an all natural
homemade one and exfoliate
your whole body! (Avoiding face
and private parts)

# Watch the sun rise or set

Wake up early, or sit outside
early evening to watch the sun.
It'll help you to feel more
energised, and peaceful.

# Donate to charity

Whether it's a few ££ here or there, or donating items such as books or clothes. It's a lovely way to give back to others, and will give you a warm feeling inside too.

# Catch up on your favourite blogs

Take some time out to browse through and comment on some of your favourite blogs. You might find some fab inspiration along the way!

# Make a Worry List

Make a list of all the things that are worrying you and take a few minutes to take some deep calming breaths and visualize the best possible outcome to each situation.

# Tell yourself why you love you

Take a long hard look in the mirror and tell yourself all the different things you love about yourself. Not just looks, but personality and quirks too!

# Start a gratitude journal

Start a little notebook, or a proper journal. Aim to write down a few things each day, appreciating the little things, and being grateful for what life has given you.

# Do something you used to love

Did you used to love to paint? Or write? Or listen to heavy metal! Think of something you used to do, and fall in love with it again!

# Breathe in the cold air

Take a few minutes and open the windows, or step outside to feel the chilly air on your face.

# Take a photo every hour

Try to take a photo every hour today, of something that has made you happy!

# Go outside barefoot

Feel the crisp, cold ground beneath your toes. Let the dew soak into your feet. Close your eyes and soak in the beautiful nature around you.

# Practise positive thinking

Find positive things to focus on today. The ability to think positively helps you cope from bad situations, limiting the duration and effect of stress.

# Spend time with a pet

Give a pet a cuddle, have a snuggle under a blanket! Or if you don't have a pet, look at cute animal photos online!

# Smile at everyone

Smile at everyone you see
today! Smiling is contagious
you know!

# Sit by a body of water

A stream, a river, a lake or even the sea! Grab a blanket and a warm drink, and just sit for a while. Listen to the sounds, watch the water flow.

# Contact people who inspire you

Look through your social media and contact or write a letter to people who inspire you, and tell them why!

# Schedule compliments

Schedule emails/calendars or even Alexa to send yourself compliments or happy messages on a regular basis. Try not to schedule in a pattern though.

# Write letters to your future self

Write letters to yourself in the future. About what's going on in your life now, what you hope your life looks like in the future. Again schedule them, or physically write them and hide them somewhere!

# Buy a plant

Treat yourself to a new
houseplant, or plant some seeds
in your garden! Plants give off
an amazing healing vibe.

# Do something you weren't allowed

Think of something you weren't allowed to do as a child, and do it! Stay up all night, eat chocolate for breakfast – you're an adult, do what makes you happy!

# Make a list

Make a list of 10 things you are proud of yourself of! Being kind hearted, raising loving children, spreading joy, reading 1000 books! Anything at all, as long as it makes you proud.

# Get Dreaming

Head over to Pinterest, and if you don't already have an account - make one! Think about a project or new change in your life you'd like to make, create some boards on Pinterest today and add lots of pins that motivate you!

Printed in Great Britain
by Amazon

36254569R00057